# Diwali

## The Hindu Festival of Lights, Feasts, and Family

*Michelle Parker-Rock*

**Enslow Publishers, Inc.**

40 Industrial Road      PO Box 38
Box 398      Aldershot
Berkeley Heights, NJ 07922    Hants GU12 6BP
USA      UK

http://www.enslow.com

*For my precious family, Larry, Gabriel, and Serene*

**Library of Congress Cataloging-in-Publication Data**

Parker-Rock, Michelle.
  Diwali: the Hindu festival of lights, feasts, and family / Michelle Parker-Rock.
    p. cm. — (Finding out about holidays)
    Summary: Introduces the history, customs, and practices of this Hindu holiday.
    Includes bibliographical references and index.
    ISBN 0-7660-2235-8 (hardcover)
    1. Divali—Juvenile literature. 2. Fasts and feasts—Hinduism [1. Divali. 2. Fasts and feasts—Hinduism.
3. Hinduism—Customs and practices. 4. Holidays.] I. Title. II. Series.
    BL1239.82.D58P37 2003
    294.5'36—dc21

                                                    2003006121

Printed in the United States of America

10 9 8 7 6 5 4 3 2 1

**To Our Readers:**
We have done our best to make sure that all Internet Addresses in this book were active and appropriate when we went to press. However, the author and publisher have no control over and assume no liability for the material available on those Internet sites or on other Web sites they may link to. Any comments or suggestions can be sent by e-mail to comments@enslow.com or to the address on the back cover.

**Photo Credits:** © 1999 Artville, Inc., p. 20; © Corel Corporation, pp. 40–41 (background); AFP/Corbis, p. 37; Amy Drewry/Associated Press, pp. i, 32; Bikas Das/Associated Press, p. 16; Cheryl Bavaro, pp. 40, 41 (insets); Chris Hellier/Corbis, p. 23; Clipart.com, p. 21, ii; Enslow Publishers, Inc., p. 5; Hemera Technologies, Inc., 6, 9 (bottom), 13 (all), 25, 31, 39 (all); http://india.purdue.org/diwali2002, pp. iii, 38; June Ponte, pp. 4, 7, 8, 10, 12, 14; Paula B. Ferazzi/Associate Press, p. 36; Photos.com, pp. 9 (top and middle), 11, 15, 42, 44, 45, 17, 18, 19, 22, 24, 27, 28, 29, 30, 34; Rajesh Nirgude/Associated Press, p. 33; Robert Holmes/Corbis, pp. 26, 35.

**Cover Photo:** Reuters New Media Inc./Corbis (main); Amy Drewry/Associated Press (top and bottom insets); Photos.com (middle inset).

# CONTENTS

Rama was born with the spirit of the god Vishnu.

Sita was born with the spirit of the goddess Lakshmi.

# The Story of Rama and Sita

Think of a holiday with firecrackers, sweet treats, and exciting tales of a prince and princess. You are thinking about Diwali, the Hindu festival of lights.

A long time ago in India, Rama (RAH-mah) was born. Rama was the oldest son of King Dasharatha (DAHSH-ah-rah). He had dark skin, dark eyes, and black curly hair. He looked like the Hindu god Vishnu. Rama was an avatar. That means he was a god born as a human. Vishnu had given Rama his spirit because Rama had a special purpose on Earth.

Rama was strong, handsome, and loved by

Lakshmi

all. He was successful in all he did. Everyone knew that he would someday become king.

In a nearby kingdom, the good King Janaka (JAH-nahk-ah) wanted his beautiful daughter, Sita (SEE-tah), to marry the bravest and strongest prince in all of India. Sita was the daughter of Earth. She was born with the spirit of Vishnu's wife, the goddess, Lakshmi (LUK-shmee). Sita was slender and graceful and had long, flowing hair. She, too, was loved by everyone.

"My daughter will marry the prince who can string my bow," said Sita's father. Many princes tried, but only Rama could string the bow. Rama and Sita had a grand wedding and lived happily for many years.

"Rama will be the next king," Rama's father said. But Rama's stepmother wanted her son,

Bharat (BHA-raht), to be king. She also wanted the king to send Rama away. The King had once promised his wife two wishes, so he told Rama to leave the kingdom.

Rama, Sita, and Rama's brother, Lakshman (LAHK-shmahn), went to live in the forest.

**Rama was the only prince who could string the bow that belonged to Sita's father.**

The forest was filled with many wild beasts and evil spirits. Rama and Lakshman fought many of them and always won.

Before long, they were visited by an evil woman. She was the sister of Ravan (RAH-vuhn). Ravan was the monster king with ten heads from the city of Lanka (LAHN-kah). When Ravan's sister saw Rama, she fell in love with him. "Marry me," she said to Rama.

"I cannot marry you," he said. "I love Sita. She is my wife." But the monster king's

Ravan's evil sister wanted to take Rama away from Sita.

8

sister did not like Rama's answer. So she tried to harm Sita. Luckily, Sita was saved by Lakshman.

Hurt and angry, Ravan's sister left the forest. But she soon returned with the evil Ravan. When Ravan saw Sita, he fell in love with her. He wanted her to be his wife. Sita said no. So Ravan tricked her and took her to his castle in Lanka.

Along the way, Sita threw her scarf and a sparkling jewel to the magical monkeys in the forest. She hoped that the monkeys would help Rama find her.

Rama and Lakshman wandered through the enchanted forest looking for Sita. Along the way, Rama met a creature that was under a magic spell. Rama freed it, and in return the creature helped Rama. It sent Rama to see

the monkey-king. "The monkey-king will help you save Sita," it said.

The monkey-king showed Rama what Sita had dropped from Ravan's flying chariot. "This is Sita's scarf and jewel," said the monkey-king. "Now go see the god of the wind. He will help you next."

Rama found the god of the wind and gave him his ring. "Show this to Sita when you see her. Then she will know that you have found her for me," said Rama.

On the way, the god of the wind met a vulture with burnt wings. The sun god had promised the vulture that his

**Ravan kidnapped Sita and took her away with him to Lanka.**

wings would grow strong again if he helped Rama. So the vulture told the god of the wind that he heard a woman in a chariot calling to Rama as she flew by. "The chariot belongs to King Ravan of Lanka," he said. The god of the wind thanked the vulture and took off again to find Sita.

The god of the wind found Sita in Lanka. He gave her the ring, and she gave him a jewel for Rama. "Tell Rama that I will not live much longer without him," she cried.

The god of the wind returned and gave Sita's jewel to Rama. "Now I will show you how to get to the kingdom of Lanka," the god of the wind told him.

With new hope, Rama crossed the miles of ocean between India and Lanka. When he arrived, he asked to see Sita. "Give me my wife, or I will destroy you," he told Ravan. But the fearless Ravan decided to fight Rama.

Ravan flew out of his castle and shot an arrow at Rama. Rama asked the gods for help.

**The monkey-king helped Rama in his quest to find Sita.**

The arrow turned around and struck Ravan's heart instead.

When Rama and Sita were together again, Rama's father appeared. He told Rama that everything had gone as planned. "This is what the gods wanted you to do," he said. "You have destroyed the evil King Ravan. Now you and Sita can return to our kingdom as king and queen."

There was a grand celebration for King Rama and Queen Sita. The royal families ordered that the cities and kingdoms be lit with rows of glittering lamps to welcome them home. Rama and Sita lived joyfully for a long time.

This is a retelling of the Ramayana (rah-MAH-yuh-nuh), the tale about Rama that has been told many times in many different

Rama and Sita lived happily together as king and queen.

ways. The holiday of Diwali reminds the people of this story of Rama and Sita.

During the festival of Diwali, thousands of little oil lamps are lit, just as they are said to have been for Rama and Sita's return. The lights are also said to welcome the goddess Lakshmi, who is said to bring gifts of wealth, good fortune, and success. That is why Diwali is also called the Festival of Lights.

There are many more things to know about Diwali. There are sweet treats and firecrackers, too. We will talk about how Diwali is celebrated in the next few chapters.

Monsoons can hurt crops and people. People give thanks when monsoon season ends.

# CHAPTER 2

# The First Diwali

The first Diwali may have been celebrated many thousands of years ago in ancient India before history was written down. At that time, many people were farmers and merchants. Merchants bought and sold what the farmers grew. The people were thankful when the monsoons, a time of very heavy rain, ended.

The people were also thankful for the crops they harvested for the New Year. A harvest is a gathering of food that is grown on farms and in gardens. The people thanked the gods for giving them a good crop.

## THE SACRED COW

*Many Hindus are vegetarians. They do not believe in killing animals to eat. Instead, rice and vegetables are eaten. Hindus believe that cows are sacred, or blessed. Cows are special to Hindus because they give milk. Milk and foods made with it, like yogurt, are important foods in India.*

Some stories say that the god Vishnu gave the people the festival of Diwali to celebrate their harvest. Today, there are farm areas in northern India where people still think of Diwali as a harvest festival.

There are other ideas about the first Diwali, too. Some people think it may have been to celebrate the marriage of the god Vishnu and the goddess Lakshmi. Others think that the

**Traditional Indian feasts are an important part of Diwali celebrations.**

holiday began like the story in Chapter 1 when Rama returns to become king. But whichever story is believed to be true, all Hindus agree that Diwali is a holiday to be enjoyed.

You may be wondering about the people who observe Diwali and the religion they follow. Who are Hindus? What is Hinduism? You will read more about this way of life in the following chapters.

**Diwali celebrates the marriage of Vishnu and Lakshmi. Here, Vishnu has four heads and arms to show that he is in the form of a god.**

**India is a large country in southern Asia. About 83 percent of the people who live in India are Hindus.**

# CHAPTER 3
# Hindus and Hinduism

**SANSKRIT**

★

*Sanskrit (SAN-skriht) is a language that was used in India a long time ago. The oldest and most blessed Hindu books are written in Sanskrit. The most important of these are the Vedas (VAY-dehs). The Vedas are holy books for Hindus—like the Bible for Christians or the Torah for Jews. The Vedas teach people how to live their lives as Hindus.*

Diwali is an important holiday to Indian Americans and Hindu people all around the globe. Hindu people believe in Hinduism, one of the oldest and largest religions in the world. It is not certain how Hinduism started, but we know that it began in the country of India over 4,000 years ago.

Many Hindus believe in a spirit called Brahman (BRAH-muhn). A spirit is an energy that does not have any shape or form. It is believed that Brahman is in all things, all the time. This means that Brahman is in all people, all animals, and all plants.

Hindus also believe that everybody has a

Many Hindus in India worship at temples, such as this one in Khajuraho.

soul or a spirit called Atman (AHT-muhn). Hinduism teaches that when a person dies, the person's soul can be born again as another person or other living thing. This is called reincarnation. How a person is reborn in the next life depends on how they live the present life. You can be born to a better life if you do more good actions than bad actions. These actions are called karma (KAHR-muh).

Hinduism is a part of everyday Hindu life. People in different parts of India and around the world practice Hinduism in many ways. Hindus can choose to study,

Praying is an important part of the Hindu religion.

pray, treat others kindly, or meditate to live a life of good karma.

Diwali is one of the main Hindu festivals. This means that it is a big religious holiday for Indian Americans and Hindu people in India and other countries. Hindus show their respect for this day in temples, at street shrines, and at

**On Diwali, many Hindu people show their respect for this day at temples.**

shrines at home. A shrine is a place where people pray.

The name "Diwali" comes from the Sanskrit word *dipavali* (dee-pah-WAH-lee). Dipavali means "row of lights." That is why Diwali is also called the Festival of Lights. On Diwali, oil lamps, candles, and colored electric lights shine brightly in Hindu homes, businesses, and temples.

**Oil lamps like this one burn during Diwali.**

Indian families welcome Diwali in lots of ways. They share many interesting stories about gods and goddesses. These stories help us to understand more about Diwali.

**Doorways are often decorated to prepare for Diwali.**

# Getting Ready for Diwali

## PUJA

*A puja (POO-jah) is a Hindu prayer service that is held in a temple or shrine. Hindu shrines can be almost anywhere. They can be in homes, in schools, in shops, or even in the street. In a shrine, there is usually a picture or statue of the god or goddess to be worshiped. During the puja, food, flowers, sweets, and holy water are offered to the god or goddess.*

Diwali comes in the Indian month of Kartika (KAH-tee-kah). It begins just before the night of the new moon. Indians use a lunar calendar. A lunar month is the time between one new moon and the next new moon. Each lunar month lasts twenty-nine-and-a-half days. This is different from the calendar used in the United States. In America, Diwali arrives at the end of October or the beginning of November.

Hundreds of thousands of families in the United States, Canada, and other countries have lots to do to get ready to

celebrate Diwali. They usually begin by making their homes very clean. They work hard at this because they believe that the goddess Lakshmi only comes to visit homes that are very clean. Lakshmi brings wealth and good fortune to clean homes.

Many families buy new clothes for Diwali. Some people choose to wear Indian-style clothes. Women and girls may choose to wear Indian saris (SAHR-eez). These are dresses made from colorful cloth that is wrapped around the body. They may also wear long, fancy shirts over baggy pants. Men and boys may wear loose-fitting shirts called kurtas (KUR-tuhz) over baggy cotton pants. Other people wear American-style dresses, shirts, and pants.

**The new moon is the time when the moon is between Earth and the sun, and looks dark to us as we look up at the sky.**

**Saris are dresses made from colorful cloth.**

People do not only shop for new clothes on Diwali. They also like to buy and wear new gold jewelry. Before they wear the new jewelry on Diwali, they perform a puja and offer it as a gift to the goddess Lakshmi.

People love to eat sweet treats and delicious foods during Diwali. Some treats are made at home, but Diwali is also a very busy time for bakeries. Barfi (BAHR-fee) is a fudge treat that is made with milk, sugar, nuts, fruits, flour, and sometimes even vegetables! Rasgullas (RAHS-GUH-lah) are milk dumplings that are dipped in sugar syrup. Jalebis (JAH-LEE-beez) is another favorite treat. A jalebis looks like a twisted pretzel. It is made from a flour batter that is fried in butter and then soaked in a sugar syrup.

During Diwali, families enjoy going out to eat. Restaurants prepare many different kinds of curried foods. Curry is a mixture of spices that is used to flavor chicken, vegetables, eggs, and other popular Indian dishes. These foods are eaten with rice and flat wheat breads called chapattis (che-PAH-teez). Pakooras (pah-KOOR-ahz) are vegetables that have been coated in chickpea flour and

**Curry is a blend of spices that is used in many Indian dishes.**

deep-fried in oil until they are golden brown. Potato samosas (sah-MOH-sahz) are little pastries filled with potatoes that are also deep-fried.

Many Indian people like to send each other Diwali greeting cards. The cards may have pictures of the goddess Lakshmi or the god Ganesh (gu-NAYSH), who is usually shown with the head of an elephant. Hindu people pray to Ganesh before starting something new. The cards wish good fortune and good luck in the New Year.

There are many things to do to celebrate this wonderful holiday. Colorful lights and tiny oil lamps are lit. Diwali is here. Now, it is time to celebrate!

**Ganesh is the Hindu god of wisdom.**

In the United States, Hindus light candles during Diwali to symbolize the "lifting of spiritual darkness," or the understanding of their faith.

# CHAPTER 5

# Diwali Is Here

Diwali is celebrated across India and in many places all around the world. In India, Diwali may last for four or five days. In the United States and Canada, it is usually only celebrated for one day. Diwali is a time for everyone to be happy. It is a time to be hopeful about the coming year.

During Diwali, businesspeople close their accounts and business books. They pay money that they owe. Then they say a special prayer called a Chopda Puja (CHOHP-dah POO-jah). They believe that the prayer brings good luck to their businesses.

## DIYA

*A diya (DEE-yah) is a traditional oil lamp made from baked clay. Before people had electric lights, they used diye (DEE-yuh)—more than one diya—on Diwali. The first diya would be lit, and it would be used to light all the other diye in the house. Some people still use diye, but candles, electric lights, or handmade lanterns like these are more common today.*

Shopkeepers may offer lower prices in their stores. Customers often purchase something made of gold or silver. They may also buy a new kitchen tool for good luck.

Many doorways to homes, shops, temples, and restaurants are decorated with colorful designs called rangoli (ran-GO-lee). Rangoli is a very old art form that uses tiny dots of colored flour to form patterns, pictures, and words on the ground. Today, powdered white stone may be used, as well. Pictures of flowers, animals, gods, goddesses, temples, and diye are common rangoli designs. Sometimes, even small footprints are drawn to welcome Lakshmi.

Lakshmi Puja (LUHK-shmee POO-jah) is performed on the night of

**Wearing new gold or silver jewelry is an important part of celebrating Diwali.**

Diwali. Prayers are said, lamps are lit, and songs are sung. Sweet treats, small puffs of rice called khil (KEEL), fruit, and flowers are offered to Lakshmi. Then to show respect, the children touch their elders' feet. Diwali pujas are held at Hindu temples and at home.

**Beautiful rangoli designs like this decorate doorways during Diwali.**

Everyone dresses in new or newly washed clothes. Some women and girls decorate their skin with henna paintings. Henna is a plant. The henna leaves are dried and ground into a powder, which is mixed with water to make a paste. The paste can be used to paint designs on the hands, feet, or other parts of the body. The designs can be simple or fancy.

Families and friends often get together

This method of henna painting is known as mehndi (MEN-dee).

during Diwali. They may attend public events where stories of the Hindu gods are told with Indian music and dancing. People visit each other at home, too. Card games are common among the adults. Activities like "Pin the Flame on the Diya" (see page 40) are fun for the children. In recent years, giving gifts has become popular, as well.

When the night of Diwali arrives, diye, candles, and electric lights are lit. The lights shine from doorways, windows, rooftops, courtyards, and gardens. The lights flicker along streets and in markets. The night glitters with the glow of all the lights of Diwali.

**Sparklers, firecrackers, and candles light up the night during Diwali.**

**Celebrating Diwali is a fun way to welcome the Indian New Year.**

When it is time for the Diwali meal, plates of tasty Indian food are shared. Sweet treats and delicious desserts are enjoyed by all. Circles of sugar called patashe (pah-TAH-shah) are a favorite candy to enjoy after dinner.

In some cities and towns, fireworks are allowed. The sky becomes bright with colorful patterns. People set off small firecrackers and light sparklers. It is believed that the loud noises of the firecrackers keep evil away.

Diwali, The Hindu Festival of Lights, may be the best-known Indian holiday. It is loved by all who celebrate it. Diwali brings joy and happiness to Hindus and Indian people each New Year.

# Diwali Project

★

## Light the Flame on the Diya

*You can make a fun game for your friends and family to play on Diwali!*

### You will need:

✔ **Orange or yellow felt**

✔ **Brown felt**

✔ **Black or white felt**

✔ **Cardboard**

✔ **Black marker**

✔ **Safety scissors**

✔ **White glue**

✔ **Yarn or string**

✔ **A scarf**

✔ **Glitter glue (optional)**

**1.** Draw the shape of a diya on the brown felt. Carefully cut it out.

**2.** Cut a piece of black or white felt so that it is the same size as your piece of cardboard. Glue the felt to the cardboard. Let it dry.

**3.** Glue the diya onto the middle of the black or white felt. Let it dry.

**4.** With the marker, draw flame shapes on the orange or yellow felt. Cut out one flame for each player.

**5.** Glue the yarn to the back of the cardboard. After the glue has dried, hang the cardboard on the wall with the felt side facing out.

**If you like, add glitter glue to make your flame sparkle!**

*How to play:*

 Give each player a flame.

 Blindfold one player at a time.

**3.** Turn the player three times as you say this rhyme:

> Diwali is the day,
> When diye light the way.
> So play this little game,
> And try to light the flame.

**4.** Each player tries to put his or her flame at the end of the wick. The winner is the person whose flame is closest to the wick!

# Words to Know

★

**Atman**—The soul of a person.

**avatar**—A human born with the spirit of a god.

**barfi**—A sweet candy made from sugar and milk.

**Brahma**—The Hindu god who is believed to have created the world.

**Brahman**—The sacred Hindu power of the universe.

**chariot**—A vehicle with two wheels that is pulled by horses.

**dipavali**—The Sanskrit word that means "row of lights."

**diya**—A clay oil lamp.

**Ganesh**—The Hindu god of wisdom.

# Words to Know

★

**Hinduism**—A religion that began in India over 4,000 years ago.

**Hindus**—People who practice Hinduism.

**jalebis**—A sweet treat that is twisted like a pretzel.

**karma**—An action that affects the form of a new life when a person is reborn.

**Kartika**—The eighth month of the Hindu calendar.

**khil**—Small puffs of rice.

**kurta**—An Indian shirt worn by men and boys.

**Lakshmi**—The goddess of riches and success.

**pakooras**—A deep-fried Indian snack.

**patashe**—A thin sugar candy.

# Words to Know

★

**puja**—A ceremony in which offerings are made to a god or goddess.

**rangoli**—Rice flour designs.

**rasgullas**—A sweet treat for Diwali.

**reincarnation**—The belief that the soul of a person can be born again.

**ritual**—A religious ceremony.

**Sanskrit**—The ancient language of India.

**sari**—An Indian dress for women and girls.

**shrine**—A holy place to pray and worship.

**temple**—A building meant for worship and prayer.

**Vedas**—Ancient Hindu religious books.

**Vishnu**—The Hindu god who saves and protects.

# Reading About

Gardeski, Christina Mia. *Diwali*. Danbury, Conn.: Scholastic Library Publishing, 2001.

Jordan, Denise M. *Diwali*. Portsmouth, N.H.: Heinemann Library, 2001.

Kadodwala, Dilip. *Divali*. New York: Raintree Publishers, 1998.

Pandya, Meenal Atul. *Here Comes Diwali: Festival of Lights*. Wellesley, Mass.: MeeRa Publications, 2001.

# Internet Addresses

★

## FamilyNYou.com: Legends of Diwali

*This fun Web sites explores the different legends behind the origin of Diwali.*
<http://www.familynyou.com/channels/
  atpdindex.php3?channel_sub_id=236>

## Time for Kids Online: Go Places—India

*This site, created by* Time for Kids, *presents a sightseeing guide, a history of India, an India facts challenge, and more!*
<http://www.timeforkids.com/TFK/specials/
  goplaces/0,12405,214513,00.html>

# Index

★

# Index